Wakefield Press

NOW–THEN

Mike Ladd was born in 1959 in Berkeley California to Australian parents and grew up at Blackwood in the Adelaide Hills. Mike is a poet, essayist and reviewer. He has published ten collections of poetry and prose, including the natural history haibun *Karrawirra Parri, Walking the Torrens from Source to Sea* (2012) and *Dream Tetras* (2022) an experimental collaboration with visual artist Cathy Brooks. Mike worked for ABC Radio for nearly forty years, firstly as a sound engineer and then as a producer of dramas and documentaries. He was the editor of Radio National's *Poetica* program, which brought Australian and international poetry to a wide audience.

NOW–THEN

New and Selected Poems

Mike Ladd

Wakefield
Press

Wakefield Press
16 Rose Street
Mile End
South Australia 5031
www.wakefieldpress.com.au

First published 2025

Supported by a grant from the Government of South Australia.

Edited by Polly Grant Butler, Wakefield Press
Text designed and typeset by Jesse Pollard, Wakefield Press

ISBN 978 1 92338 821 5

A catalogue record for this book is available from the National Library of Australia

Wakefield Press thanks Coriole Vineyards for continued support

Versions of some of these new poems have previously appeared in the *Adelaide Review*, *Antipodes*, *Australian Poetry Journal*, *Axon Creative Explorations*, *Best Australian Poems*, the *Canberra Times*, *Cordite*, *InDaily*, *Island*, *Meanjin*, *Meniscus*, *Plumwood Mountain Journal*, *Red Room*, *Saltbush Review*, *Saturday Paper*, *Verity La*, and *Westerly*. My sincere thanks to the editors.

Contents

Foreword

Poetry began for me in early childhood. I have a clear memory of my maternal grandmother bathing me in a tub and chanting in her high, wispy voice:

'swim Sam swim
swim across the dam
swim like a swan.'

The rhythm of those words synchronised with the swishing water and their dense alliteration and rhyming imprinted on me. I think most people are receptive to this kind of language, but I've sometimes wondered if there's a poetry gene carried by certain individuals that predisposes them to be more than usually sensitive to it. Many of the poets I know have a particular mind frame, a way of being in the world, haunted by words. I began hearing phrases in my head and writing them down as small, fragmentary poems at about eight or nine years old. Tendencies like this can be scorched or nurtured, depending on your parents. Mine were nurturers.

My grandfather was a Presbyterian minister and a closet poet. At the age of sixteen, I inherited his poetry library, mostly the English Canon from Blake to Yeats, but including some contemporary poets like Yevtushenko. That same year, a rejection letter, four pages long, handwritten, and full of affirmation from Rodney Hall, poetry editor of the *Australian*, made me begin to think of myself as a poet.

An early love of the poetry of Robert Frost and Wilfred Owen led onto T.S. Eliot, Allen Ginsberg, Michael Dransfield and Seamus Heaney.

I began to read poets in translation too, key among them Miroslav Holub, Wisława Szymborska and Nazim Hikmet. I also liked the ancient Greek epigrammatists, the Japanese poets Basho and Issa, and Arthur Waley's translations of the ancient Chinese poets.

While still a teenager I found my way to the *Friendly Street* poetry readings initially held at Gordon Sym Choon's ex-fireworks factory in Union Street, central Adelaide. There I met mentors-by-example in such writers as John Bray, Andrew Taylor, Richard Tipping, Kate Llewellyn and Peter Goldsworthy. I joined the Poets' Union which led to contact with a wider group of contemporary poets from New South Wales and Victoria such as ΠO and the *9-2-5* group. In 1984 the Friendly Street collective published my first book of poems.

I finished a Bachelor of Arts degree in English and Philosophy at Adelaide University, studying as much modern Australian and American poetry as I could, but decided academe wasn't for me and opted for joining a punk new-wave band, followed by overseas travel, sound recording in west Africa and a career in radio. For nearly twenty years I was coordinating producer and presenter of *Poetica* on ABC Radio National, which gave me the opportunity to meet and record many of Australia's best poets as well as a wide range of overseas poets.

It's over forty years since my first book appeared, which seems a good enough motivation to bring out this *Selected Poems.* Back in 1984, even a debut poetry collection by a twenty-five-year-old received a dozen reviews, including in the mainstream press. Today, poetry seems more marginalised than ever. It exists as a kind of self-help society where poets who recognise each other's affliction form small groups, not to kick the habit, but to encourage it. Low ratings, and yet it survives, as Auden said, 'in the valley of its making' and sometimes, somehow, it travels much further.

Looking back over the last forty years, I notice periods of influence on my work from the east European minimalists, an interest in Asian forms such as the pantun, the haibun and the lüshi, a bit of postmodernism, and more experimental, or more traditional phases. There have been a few tweaks. Sometimes it takes a decade or two to see what's needed in a poem. Didn't Pierre Bonnard continue to alter his paintings years after they had been sold and were hanging on someone else's walls? Maybe what we make is never really finished – it just ends when we run out of time.

*

The 'New Poems' in this collection date back as far as 2016. I'm a deliberately slow worker. They have appeared in various newspapers and magazines but haven't been collected in a book before. They cover a period when the environment is paying us back for our continuing abuse of it, a time of fires and floods, pandemic, warfare and tyranny. So far, the 2020s make it hard to keep your faith in humanity, but I suppose you could say that about nearly every decade. It's been a time when friends and family have died, so there are a few elegies. There are also road trips and further travels and poems about art and artists and the extraordinary ability of the natural world to still surprise us with joy.

I would like to thank Ken Bolton and his *Lee Marvin Readings* which were a source of inspiration and motivation, and all the poets I have workshopped the new poems with: Peter Lach-Newinsky, Susan Hampton, Jelena Dinic and the Metropole Poets, John Jenkins and Arthur Giannopoulos. Thanks also to my long-term collaborator Cathy Brooks who provided the cover artwork, and to Michael Bollen of Wakefield Press, for his continued support of my writing.

Mike Ladd
2025

New Poems

Palaeontology/Archaeology

At twelve, I wanted to be a palaeontologist
digging up bones in the paddocks round here,
easing a scythe of jaw from the creek bank –
not Diprotodon, but horse. Still,
I remember the thrill carrying it home
through that raw suburb, layered now in my mind.

Those strange creatures that evolved there:
Mr F. tuning his finicky engines,
Mrs H. axing the heads off chooks
their beaks still gaping on the bloody stump,
Mr B., a grey floppy hat among bean rows,
Mrs P. parading in her negligee
and beating her son with a hose.

In bed at night I pegged ancient shallow seas,
looking for life stamped in stone,
the dream coins of fossil joy.
And now there's not enough time,
I want another go –

Digging under this new estate,
a chaconne of grey mortgages,
I would excavate the swamp that was here:
a gift of water where blue cranes
teetered into their westering
and the moon behind them rose from the weeds.

I would sort and classify those sounds:
the dour claxon of the crane,
the crickets and frogs still calling
from the storm drain.

Shall I dig further?
Past the middens of the Kaurna,
proving their earlier claim,
exposing old theft and murder.

Where is my heartland?
What if I dug clear through the earth,
emerging in Skara Brae,
that Orcadian flint in my family?
What if I climbed from the harbour at Kirkwall,
entered that shop with the soundless bell,
stood at the bench where great-grandfather Flett
finesses ships' chronometers and doesn't look up?
His clock faces stilled to stone.

Would these people want me back?
Should you lie down with ancestor bone?

Moonrise in a New Suburb

Colourbondage:
fences edging the raw lowness.

On this street
Google maps can't find yet

a full moon
has just been released.

Seems no one else saw it
jump the rooftops –

all the TV lights
through curtain cracks.

Over waste ground
winter green,

a moon
on parole.

The Corpse Flower Sketch

(for John Berger)

Sunset, climate-warmed and volcanic –
in the hot sky
a giggle and crake of fruit bats
flown south from development
print themselves in the old-money trees
of spooked Park Terrace mansions –
the corpse flower is blooming tonight.

In the Botanic Gardens queues
strobed with phone flashes
shuffle under the captive palms
and Titan Arum releases its smell;
part dog bone, part teenage sweat shoe.
A velvety, visceral purple,
pleated curtain around a creamy phallic spike.

John Berger died today in outer Paris;
two more species disappeared somewhere in the world.
After sketching this flower
I will go home and read his *Photocopies* again,
his portraits of ingenious non-celebrity.
Which reminds me it was here, in this opera house
of tropical plants, I last saw my aunt alive.

A stenographer to Menzies,
she kept those secrets.
But on that final outing she told us snippets
of her single woman's life:

a personal assistant at the Southern Cross Hotel,
the manager made her cut up the bedsheets the Beatles slept in
so he could sell little squares to the fans.

We came up this walkway over the lotus pond
and met a bird, a kingfisher flown from who knows where.
Stopping her there in her ninetieth year,
smiling at its magical quality.
Something Berger would have drawn if he were there.
Not a word, but an acknowledgement.
The crowded forest grows inside now.

Prove That You are Human

Select all squares with crossings.

The blue wheel goes round.

This park looks familiar
and I had a bicycle just like that.
I wonder where the motorbike rider is going?
Maybe to his long-lost mother's house.
They've only just rediscovered each other
after a lifetime of separation.

Select all squares with traffic lights.

That woman sitting on the bench
behind the stop sign,
she's a refugee who's spent years
trying to prove she's human.

Select all squares with clouds.

including clouds with silver linings
and clouded judgements.
Every square has clouds.
Is that a metaphor?

Prove that you are a human.

Do something lovely
or vicious
or both.

Select all images with stairs.

The young man going up those back stairs
is on his way to a click farm,
a windowless building in
a street without a minimum wage.
He's paid a pittance to plant
likes and follows and five-star reviews.

To continue, type the characters
you see in the picture.

What language is this?
Those twisted cat scratchings
look like my failed drafts.

The blue wheel goes round
and round.

I'm not a robot.

Please believe me.

Plasticland

At the edge of the car yard
the bunting in
cloudless
air

framed by two poles
triangular flags
clap in the
wind

lift,
flutter,
clap again:

petro-chemical colours
the retina
loves

the shape, feel and
hue of our
times

styrofoam grains
in our salt and
blood

Hard pebbles of plastic
churn in the guts
of seabirds

a million waves

from

here.

A Minute's Silence

Stopped in an Italian grocery
between eleven and a minute past

I fell into a white-faced clock –
arrived in a silent classroom:

my head bowed to a wooden desk,
a smell of lost time and crayon wax.

Outside early heat paling the grass,
the demountable sky.

Flags, teachers, monitors, anthems.
But come back now

to the radio bugling the Last Post
between imported jars,

this still profusion:
grindstones of pecorino,

cannoli flaunting
their creamy innards.

There, a guy restless to pay,
thinking it's all jingoistic crap.

There, behind the counter,
a young woman in a hijab.

There, a family
standing to attention.

There, some people ducking out the door
to save the minute.

At the going down of the sun,
the dark blood sausage,

and in the panini
we will remember them.

Portrait of a Widower

(cleaning up after a storm)

All calm now as he sweeps the drive.
The garden radio (a beaten transistor)
plays *Wild is the Wind* by Nina Simone.

Tree bark like torn sleeves,
discarded sashes from a race,
piles in front of his broom.

He finds a nest like a nebula.
Inside, the core felted to cup an egg.
Some small life began here before the storm.

Like a leaf clings to a tree, Oh my darling cling to me,
For we are creatures of the wind . . .
Nina's voice, a deep, burnished moan.

Last night, he walked the streets
as the wires were clashing, branches snapping
bins blown banging along the road

returning in the small hours to this shocked house
from which she has
irretrievably, gone.

On Reading My Own Obituary in a Deli by the Airport

There it was in the Sunday Mail: 'Mike Ladd (pictured)
one of S.A.'s three best poets and a good bloke. Vale.'
Short, sweet, and wrong. Or was it? What if I had died
and this was the afterlife? A deli by the airport.
Balfours' pies, Farmers' Union Iced Coffee
mixed lollies and the Sunday Mail: Forever!
Outside the sun was shining. Some daffodils
were poking up through the scrappy front lawns
the dogs were minding their fences
and the cars kept swishing past, pretty much as usual.
Not too exciting, but it could be worse.
The Vietnamese lady behind the counter
asked me if there was anything else I wanted:
More poems, more prizes, more kisses,
more spices, more species, more vistas, more vastness,
more amour – more and more and more.
But I didn't say that. Just thanked her and walked
through the plastic strips on the door.

Isolation

It's cold out there.
Rain just scribbled static through
the bare branches of the apricot tree
leaving buds of pure light.
Hunkered down, pandemic-still,
there's time to watch the beads of water form,
then fall.

Isolation is nothing new in this sequestered street.
I think of black-aproned Maria
who fed the magpies white shapes of bread
and crumbs of Greek.
I haven't seen her for some time . . .
'Maria died a year ago.
We thought you knew.'

A thread of glass
connects us to a cloud,
but who would choose a virtual life?
The physical keeps me sane.
A pause between showers –
a chance to prune my vine.

Two weeks later. The borders are still closed
though not to bees. They dance
through cups of scented light
in the apricot tree. The sky, a shimmer blue.
I relearn my garden, my village
and hardest of all, my self,
this closer view.

Apple Picking in Plague Time

The sky is freed from planes
and birdsong trickles clear,
birds worship the still air:
picking apples in plague time.

The trees signal with their arms
which ache with ripened fruit,
fallen crowds rot underneath:
picking apples in plague time.

There is more here than I can eat
bags will be left on front steps,
notes scribbled if doors stay shut:
picking apples in plague time.

Newton home from Cambridge
escaping the Black Death,
found gravity universal:
picking apples in plague time.

At night I dream an orchard
and see us Eden naked,
what gives life also takes it:
picking apples in plague time.

Passing the House

(i.m. Ann Newmarch)

In Beatrice Street the dog and I
face west. The bottom of the sky

is a fluoro-orange band
under indigo curtains coming down.

No matter how brightly you glow
a moment later you're gone.

The night is still. The swamp oak
in her garden makes no sound.

The pool is empty but for July rain,
a splash of party voices only imagined.

I thought I saw a light on upstairs –
the merest chink in the drawn blinds.

A willed mistake. Her art remains –
her eye and aching, accurate hand

but her joy and mayhem are all gone –
she does not haunt her gate as I do now.

Time to go home – the dog wants
his biscuits and his bone.

M.R.I

Embedded in the white dome,
your tubular sarcophagus –
tune to *Radio Underworld.*

Magnetic pulses like Philip Glass
fight Schubert in the headphones
wildly out of key. . .

Focus. In the slow movement
of the String Quintet
become an albatross.

Lock wings and glide
a thousand miles without a beat
south of Tristan

wave after wave passing below,
the reverse Antarctic wind
in your wide white span.

The Repaired Spine

It's nearly dawn.
Pain, against my will,
makes me a bore
giving too many details over the phone.
There's a loneliness to it
though it's the most common thing
in the world.

At least it's brought me this stillness.
I stare out the window
to watch the world form
grey shapes from blackness.

Pain triages my life.
It clarifies friends,
resets me to family, food,
loved one, meds.

The early news is full of it.
Pain much worse than mine
written on faces in Gaza,
faces in Ukraine.

Some pain is hard to learn from.
But this has taught me about the Other,
to reach into the fragile stuff
from which we're made.

Saying goodbye to pain is such treasure.
With repaired spine to sit once more
beside you in the kitchen, to simply
talk and laugh
and brew some coffee on the stove.

How slow I've been to speak of joy.
But I now find it here, pouring in the window
with the light under the grapevine.

What the Creek Said

The creek chuckled
recalling me falling into it
aged four
throwing a stick
and forgetting to let go.

The creek sighed, reminding me:

I didn't kiss Lizzy Harris
when I had the chance

I wasn't there
for my father's last days

and tyrants still rule the world.

The creek murmured that I've lost:

a cane-handled umbrella

a black bicycle

a best friend.

The creek wanted
me to get back:

the ability to take a high mark
in a game of football

faith that the world can be made fairer.

The creek said
that for itself
it would like restored:

the little swamp where it rested

the banjo frogs

the natural balance as it was
before the Industrial Revolution.

The creek would like that
very much.

Weed Spell

Vetch and cress,
sorrel,
mustard,
purslane,
spurge.

Wort and mallow,
dodder,
nettle,
fennel,
furze.

Couch and pigweed,
groundsel,
goosefoot.
ox-eye,
burrs.

Flax and goatsrue,
ripgut,
fleabane,
Paterson's
curse.

Blend
on hillside,
mix in river,
spread and
scourge.

Flying in Over the Coorong

Below us,
the marbled endpapers
of that great book:
the Murray

I'm nearing home –
but this sweetness is
strangled:
blind greed stops the fishes' mouths,
starves the waders

their heart beats
on the shore
gone.

A glaring stillness.

The plane is prepared for landing,
pressure mutes
the eardrums.

Sun on the mirrors'
interlocking shimmer,
calligraphy of lakes flowing on
one to another

the strand,
the braid,
the wild seaward shore –

a terminal line of breakers

Boomer Beach Adolescence

The streets dive-bomb into the sea
and the girls are in the shacks
and we, starved for their touch,
unaware of our own beauty,
can't believe our luck
as we drive our wrecks here.

The waves curl and dump –
an exquisite series
of punches to the heart,
the gulls blanket the roofs,
and little white snails
live and die in the scrub

fragile under us
as our first real kisses
stun our mouths.

Persistence of the She-oak

When this she-oak fell in a storm
it lifted a profile of stone –
tiles and laths of the dry earth's roof.

Its roots raised green shale,
red-gold sandstone,
a little reef.

Now the tree lives horizontally,
its leeside anchors
hooked in the ground.

There's a fertile rust on its tassels,
endless wind and sea in them –
sea that formed the stones.

I will never get over she-oaks,
their cragginess thatching
that sound.

Echidna

Undulant pinecone,
needle-nose sniffer,

I imagine you mountain-size,
monstering a city.

You are harder to pick up than Hungarian,
more stand-offish than a stylite saint.

Little high judge in your wig of thorns,
its pattern complex as a deal in the Senate,

once a year
you queue for spiky sex

then crash burrow-wards
through the bracken curtain.

You are distant as Aldebaran.
Private as euthanasia.

Whipbird

A whipbird draws back its sling
and fires a pebble of sound.
Ghosts of mist fly up the valley.
At last, some thinking ground.

The Point

By the rail at Echo Point
I took a photo on a day
when everything was gone:

crags,
waterfalls,
blue haze of eucalypts,
any sense of distance.

The mist so total
even sound was missing.

A young couple beside me
leant on the edge,
the fog condensing
tiny jewels
in their hair.

Thinking of old Chinese prints
I pointed my lens at random,
fooling myself
I was taking a photo of the void.

Later I stared into
the image spread on a screen –
abstract billows
of white and grey.

Then I found a dot,
a speck of dust on the glass
that wouldn't brush off.

Blowing up the image,
I saw the dot had wings.

Perhaps a pilot bird,
hard to tell,
but a presence
finding its way through.

It looked like music:

a breve
escaping the stave

The Quince

Staring at the dark.
Moonlight on the quince blossom.
A new galaxy.

Lüshi

He wanted to get life into the painting,
though he realised he was part of the view.
The image could never hold its own outside.
He kept at it. Life did too.

When artists die, their kids get lumbered
with lots of packing up to do.
Most of his work went in the skip,
but, they saved a few.

Night Patrol

Sometimes in the silent house
I wake to sounds that don't exist.
In the held breath of the kitchen
my dead father makes a sandwich.

On my patrol at 2.40 a.m.
long-gone children play in their dressing gowns –
they don't see me as I step through their game.
The dog snores, though he's underground.

A Little Elegy

He was an escaped party-balloon
caught in the bare spikes of a tree.
Doomed, wonderful,
all gas and hilarity.

A lightness we would watch
die gradually that season.
Grateful though for his refusal
of all that numbing reason.

A Little Love Poem

When you take off your high heels,
when you step out of your power dress,
when my work clothes lie slain on the floor
and your head rests on my chest,

then we slowly become our just selves
and stroke each other human:
and it's fire, forest, cave,
savannah, again.

Lake Waskesiu

This is where we swam, father,
gold-green in close-shore light.
Climbing up the bank, I put my foot
in a hornets' paper dome and the swarm
chased me through the woods,
a cartoon cloud with a fiery sting.

In the white season, you and I came back
to walk the surface frozen thick.
We were out far when we found the blood,
the fresh brown shape of half a deer –
wordlessly we understood,
turned together, and ran.

Decades later, restrained in a ward,
in a bare room,
on a mattress
on the floor
(lake ice adrift)
the beast caught you.

Ate your mind alive.

My Mother and the Whirlwind

It starts casually,
a funnel of dust in the quivering air –

grows into an old-testament giant
spinning in a cloak of sticks and torn grass.

Deepening red, the spout moves forward,
a genie dancing, arms held above its head.

My mother, a little girl in a drab summer dress
stands in the same paddock.

Up close, the vortex is half the sky.

She runs, is lifted mid-step into the dance,
the rapture of the air.

Her grey dress spins out,
turning and turning, Sufi ecstatic.

She is a swallow.
She is a page torn from a bible.

Then (the wind dying suddenly)
she's dropped on top of a water tank.

She creeps back inside the house
through the flywire door.

Her mother, unaware,
scolds her for the dirt on her dress

And just look at your hair . . .

Last Days of the Blockbuster

The palette of Degas
an abstract before its time.

Manet's moon.
Seurat's grass.

The clouds, the snows
the rooftops.

Pissarro's green dreaming
under boughs –

these are the last days
of the blockbuster.

'You can't see it
until you stand back'

says my old mother
leaning on my arm.

Monet's same church
in fifteen different lights.

We don't exit
through the gift shop:

'I've got more postcards than I could ever use'
she says, 'even a calendar is risky.'

If this was a film
Bach unaccompanied cello

would start playing
over the credits.

We go back
against the flow

'It wasn't much up close
but now I see the reflections.'

The sky in the water.
The last bit of light.

Night Flight

Morphine pump. Call button.
Our flight deck glows
green and purple
and phosphor yellow.
On this long haul
to the unknown continent
you are the captain,
me, copilot in the chair beside you.

A lethal injection
would be supersonic
but we must take the slow way:
on Morphine Air
there are many delays,
waits on the tarmac,
the engines outmoded and cranky.

But we are approaching –
I can feel your new, strange land
over the horizon,
a great, dark mass
separated from us
by a thin disc of dawn.

You have nearly flown us there.

Apricity

(i.m. Meg Ladd)

The week she died
her camellias never looked better.
She and her beloved
planted them sixty years ago –
Tsar, Coquette, Champagne.

They were responding with urgency –
El Niño had begun,
as her breathing
grew fast and shallow.

The blackbird
(for so many years
her spirit-familiar)
called for her repeatedly,
nervous
the back doorstep
was empty.

There were no crusts on the lawn –
he could no longer hop beside her
when she dug the soil
in this garden.

Now the backyard fills with winter sun.

The bird comes back.

So has she gone? Has she gone?

Stella Bowen Self-portrait

That enormous right eye
centres the painting.

Lit-up amber, it's a caution,
a statement about seeing.

Warm light falls on the right side of her face,
a fineness of chestnut hair –

I could almost place my hand
into the picture

stroke that hair just above her temple
knowing exactly how it would feel.

Her stare unsentimental,
she remembered her hometown:

'a queer little backwater of intellectual timidity,
prettyish, banal and filled to the brim with an anguish of boredom.'

Mills Terrace, North Adelaide.
Tennis and roses, church and servants, and heat.

*

Now I imagine she's not looking in a mirror
but at me, her viewer.

She's just caught me fudging the truth
or stuck in some small-mindedness.

I am judged
and found wanting.

But I turn the gaze back to its real subject,
the gazer herself.

Anger tightens her jaw.
Is she thinking of lost time,

how she demoted herself
to housekeeper for Ford Madox Ford,

her painting pushed back behind his novels
while she cooked and dealt with the bills?

Is she thinking of his new, younger woman
taking her place as she once took another's?

Now she stares into the face of the Great Depression,
thirty-six years old, a daughter to support

her life in Paris disappearing
with the exchange rate.

She sees the rise of the dictators,
her old friend Ezra spruiking Mussolini.

She sees how she must hawk herself
doing family portraits of the rich who are still rich –

but this one
is just for her.

She looks hard into the future:
a Second World War, survival in England,

perhaps all the way to her own death,
not enough money in the bank to come home –

finally wanting again the *'sky almost empty of blue'*
'the yellow ochre of the dried grass.'

* Quotations are from Stella Bowen's memoir *Drawn from Life*

Clarice Beckett: *Silent Approach*

He arrives before and after sound:
the slave hum of the morning traffic,
the magpie's liquid medicine.

He is antiphon –
comes from grey out of grey
soft as mist print.

And is he a she
or neither,
or perhaps not human at all?

What is it that approaches silently?
Is it another world calling
in the shape of a walker?

A figure that is not substance,
but a gap through which to escape
this foggy suburban day

on a random stroll
beside slap-dash shrubbery
and the power poles?

Joss by Cheng Ran and Item Idem

Run at the illusory stairway,
    the chemical sun –
burn a paper model of this world:
    it appears for real
in the wispy hands of the dead.

What will you send?
    a humble beer and pizza,
    her favourite chair,
    the smokes that killed him?

How will it taste and feel there
    between the rungs
    of disappearing light?

Papery gold,
    the flying ash of credit cards,
    open only a moment
    the door to the burning mansion.

Representation

Wearing straw hats and an air of privilege
unchanged since the '50s,
the private schoolgirls at The Art Gallery
have escaped from a Charles Blackman.

Now it's pouring
we shelter under the Welcome Plaza perspex roof
while the warm rain drums.
Upritchard's giant figures stand over us,
a cast lizard on a leg, a bird on a head –
No, the bird is real, and turns to look.

The rain dimples Slessor's mythic harbour
in rainbow Gadigal land.
The warships are still there, grey shapes in the mist,
but no drowned Joes drift past, only brown jellyfish
and a hint of diesel slicking the tide.

On the bus home
the kids curate themselves on their phones.

The Eyre Highway

A candy stripe of road in good-season green,
dreaming track of the grey nomad:
Viscount, Windsor, Franklin, Vista,
towed into a horizon of Mallee
then treelessness, the caravanserai of the Great Bight.

On the Nullarbor a delicatessen of flowerings
among the calcrete:
eremophila, hakea, muelleriana, ptilotis, Sturt's pigface.

Vanguard, Scenic, Sundowner, Island Star,
the caravans refuel, pass the whales rolling
in cold blue, blowing their heart-shaped breaths
against the cliffs.
The westward procession, Port Augusta to Norseman,
the clockwise cycle:
Roma, Coromal, Paramount, Supreme.

Banggarla to Wirangu, Wirangu to Mirning,
under the highway the caves sounding,
Anangu law still there.

The Huon Highway

Pretty as a pippin and just as tight –
land of honesty boxes
and shot holes in the signage.
Woods culture of stiff opinion:
log and lop / love and lock.
Square houses, their squiggles of smoke
tanging the valley.
A road from big to small:
storm clouds hazing the Hartz mountains,
in the tidy glens, a wrenish attention to detail.
All double lines:
massacre of possum and pademelon,
gut stink in the roadside daisies.
The blackberries ripen by the river
which starts out Scots and English,
finishes sweepingly French –
and the Melukerdee,
where are their names?

The Great Northern Highway

Perth so far behind and Port Hedland's murdered country.
Broome smells of frangipani and acrid smoke,
sounds of crows and whistling kites and turbo props
lining up the airport down the tin barrel of the street.
Wealthy whites, pearly whites, old whites on tours.
Red sand and milk crates of the black town camp:
an apartheid smouldering at the dump.
Past Derby, the fineness of bauhinia, corymbia,
pindan and kurrajong, understory of dry-season grass.
Brutalities of numberplates: F I F O, 'Fit In or Fuck Off.'
Oppressive conformism pretending to be larrikin.
Red road train on a red road.
Boab's upturned tap root into the blue.
Salties moving far inland, pushed by higher tides.
Termite mounds, morphing into ancestors at twilight,
brown-red sepulchres or lions in their prides.
The names need reclaiming.
Why King Leopold Range? Old slaver and hand-chopper.
And Lord Kimberley, who is he to overwrite the land?
The real names are in the rock crevices and caves:
Windjana, Jandamurra, Imintji: kingfisher country.
At Warmun, Queenie McKenzie painted the massacres,
a Gija human worth less than a bullock on that frontier.
Now Rover Thomas's owl-dreaming looks down from the wall
at steak and chips in the roadhouse café.
Stopping on a side-track tonight, all still, all silent.
Moon snow on the boab. Then, a curlew cry.

Climbing Rwetyepme

Only the wind in acacias and spinifex,
the grind and clink of our footsteps
in the dark.

Mars setting below us,
a red new moon on the rise.
Orion, Taurus, The Seven Sisters
slowly erased from the skies.

This wrongskin woman
pregnant to a forbidden man
lies down in stone,
hands resting above her swollen belly,
waiting for a birth that will not come.

We pass the knees,
the thighs,
reach the distended navel.

Then the sun breaks
the waters of the world.

The Fire Enters Fairy Dell

White flakes fall, a breeze picks up,
the valley fogs with grey.

A forest kingfisher spotlit
by halogen-yellow sun
preys on moths escaping –

then flits as well.

The orange dancers come;
the quivertrees.

Black crescents spiral down that once
were green lance tips in the sky.

Two wattle birds still chase and squabble
though their territory's alight.

The elemental is here.
It has a strange beauty –
heresy to call it so.

Up on Chatsworth Road,
neighbours with hose and rake
collectivise their firebreak.

A pendulum of water bomb
swings from a chopper's underside –
a wrecking ball for flame.
Unseen, god-like, the pilot
leaves in a throbbing arc.

Up on the ridge
fire trucks pulse carmine and blue
into dancefloor smoke
that came from crowds of eucalypts.

And now it's fully dark.

The stumps are glowing in Fairy Dell
like lanterns on a Shinto path.

Haze

The prime minister's words fill the air –
they hang over the bays,
obscure the roads to the little towns,
drift
between the bridge's cables.
His words
turn the sunlight dirty orange.
You need a breathing mask
to get through them.
We are longing for a downpour
to wash the prime minister's words away.

Meanwhile, what he refuses to say
keeps burning

Four Seasons of the Oreades

High shimmer of blue. This summer
no smoke drifts through the Mountain Ash glade,
no flame but sunfall on memory's blackened trunks.
The forest kingfisher lords it over his tangled realm.
Eucalyptus Oreades, named for nymphs
who appear and dissolve
in cross-hatched strokes of limb and light.
The forest echo – voices repeating
the ends of phrases, the shapes of leaves.
Multitudinous murmurings.

❋

White and brown verticals of autumn Oreades –
a forgotten marina,
sails hanging in ribbons from the masts.
Halyards and hawsers of the stilled fleet
strew indefinite paths.
After a week of rain
an ephemeral stream appears in the glade
and white foam bubbles at the trees' feet.
A lyrebird scratching sweet, wet earth,
leaps up and away, trailing feathered curves like bark.

❋

The powerful owl waits on his icy perch,
watching for footfall to print the path
or movement on a powdered branch.

Silence. A few flakes falling.
Winter guardian of the Oreades,
chevroned burnt wood and white,
a stare, unremittingly cold.
The snow fallen on bark litter below
repeats his feathers' pattern.
The undergrowth still, halo bright.

❋

At the feet of Oreades
white stars of fringe myrtle
spice the air this spring
and a warming breeze clatters the rigging –
the forest is ready to sail,
has somewhere to go.
Down a barely perceptible path
the regent bowerbird has built
the glade in miniature.
His churring gold lights up the gloom.

Flood

Barbers' chairs turn slowly in the current,
dummies in bridal white are baptised
in the brown, uncontrollable river.

Blindly the flood reads its way through the bookshop,
prises open cabinet drawers in Centrelink
and blurs the files.

In the Crystal Shop it muddies the facets,
adds shit notes to the essential oils.

The wood from the lumberyard heads downstream
the way it used to do in red cedar days.

Afterwards, lower stories vomit their insides out,
line the pavements with a white-goods spume.

Through the town there's a line drawn
on windows and walls.
Friends help mop up. Some stay, some go.
Fans aerate the shells of shops.

A notice in the jeweller's: *After thirty years*
I was beaten by a raindrop. All commissions
will be honoured. It may take time.

I have your names but some are now illegible.
Please call this number. . .

The swamp oaks make ambiguous sighs
drawing in the water left rippling at their feet.

Paddy Field, Ubud

The daily offering is left at the crossroad.
This oblong of water channels
frames two bodies, both stripped.
One works on a tan, one on planting rice.

A luxury villa built in the middle of the paddy
promises an authentic experience;
cocktails in the plunge pool
while watching the sweating farmer.

Units of income, units of service.
White bodies burn in the light,
wrecking the thing they say they love:
the paddy gets eaten.

High up, jets glint over the young green,
over the boys still practicing their kite flying –
the distant international roar
of arrival and all that departs.

The Frangipani Collector

He reaches up with a cleft bamboo rod.
A flick of the wrist,
and down tumbles
a flake of cream and yellow,
a five-petalled spiral
drawing the eye
into its axial zero.

His little propellers of perfume
will decorate the tables and bedsheets
of tourists, then be swept
into the bin.
Does he think while collecting,
'Was this why we fought for independence?
to be their servants again?'

Every job has its mastery;
if he twists the rod just so
each bloom drops down like Bali snow.
Unbruised, untorn,
perfectly folded whiteness.
If not, it sticks in the cleft
and doubles his work.

A wedding or a feast
is a long morning,
is hours of his life
evaporating in the scented heat.
He shoulders his rod,
this fisherman in shallow skies,
a presence lingering long after he's gone.

Until Java

Into the hotel room floats
a little reality –
the smell of warm dung.

A missing brick in the wall –
peering through
I see two cows in their byre.

Sleek, caramel-coloured,
happy as Hathor,
the disc of the sun between their horns.

Pungency of birth and death
no incense can cover.
Safe here in Bali, until shipped to Java.

In the banana glade
a rooster cries
in irreverent red.

Java Suite

Under the transmitter towers
a papaya garden
receiving rain.

A thousand silent swallows came.
From you,
no message.

Feeling for the right stone
in opaque water –
fish-trap building.

Banana tree –
green flag
on a hill of plastic.

Its whole life
without a shred of waste –
the Java sparrow.

Occasional Tremors

That's not the Shinkansen coming in
or a rock concert crescendo –

that's the whole tarred-over earth
having a little shimmy.

The bass note
goes right through your spine.

Don't rattle those dishes at me:
I know I haven't done them yet.

The map gets crinkled
by deeper routes.

In the after-silence one word echoes:
Surface. Surface. Surface.

Phrasebook

Are you lost?
Show me how to play.
Tomorrow is my last day here.
I'll send you copies of the photographs.
It's like feeding daisies to the pigs.
If you ever visit Scotland come and stay.

It's longer than a day without bread.
How do you say that in Basque?
Do you like it when I do this?
Is this the bus to Cordoba?
I am the flying god of sunflowers.
You won't get it if you have to ask.

The Cat of Lisbon

The cat of Lisbon listens in its sleep –
the summer rustles outside
and a Marcha band
echo-locates the street.
When gulls cry from the Tagus,
the cat's ears flick –
its ancestors went
with Cabral and Da Gama
down that estuary,
ratcatchers in Macau, Timor,
Goa and Brazil – riches
shining there like a sardine's belly.

The cat of Lisbon is a white tabby,
a fine dark streak either side of its spine,
leopard spots like an old azulejo
from Mozambique.
A cat full of *saudade,*
it knows there's another self
on a balcony it can never reach,
even if it balanced on the washing lines
and leapt the centuries.

Wearing Other Poets' Clothes

When the Brooklyn sun
was burning my scalp
David Cortes gave me his light tan Stetson –
UNITE! Union of Needle Trades
and Textile Employees the inside label said.
I wore it as we crossed the vaulted
harp-string bridge,
the water glittering below
and the Mexicans playing soccer in the park
on the Brooklyn side.

One dusk August Kleinzahler
lent me a green plaid hunting jacket
as the fog came in on a fine San Francisco day
chilling everything suddenly
like the door left open
on an ocean-sized freezer.
'Keep it,' he said as I left his house.
It fitted me well
a bit ambiguous, a bit Village People,
some guys sizing me up
on the trolley home to Geary Street.

Now that I think of it, I have
a knapsack belonging to Basho,
a scarf from Robert Frost
and a fine red umbrella of Nazim Hikmet's.
Yeats left my grandfather

a pair of black leather brogues
which he handed me down
but they pinched my feet
so I gave them to the Salvos.

On the Frozen River

A warm spell
had run down the thawing river

the current buckling and lifting
a junkyard of ice

then it set hard again
in the starry frost that night.

No adults to watch us
we skidded down the bank –

we entered transparent houses,
peered through panes and jambs and frames.

There was a glass stegosaurus
with sun shining through its vanes.

Cracks appeared under our boots –
we knew the day was beginning its erasure.

The ice groaned as it shifted.
It warned us with a low goodbye.

Soon
we could no longer walk in this world.

Bolivian Mountain Miniatures

On the mountain,
a red-capped woodpecker.
In the valley, someone hammering.
Not quite together.

*

Over there, a young man
guards the radio masts –
a dog for company
and the voices in the wires.

*

The 'express bus'
is always in first gear.
The driver crosses himself
three times before he starts.

*

There is up or down.
There is no across.
You assess carefully
the journey's value.

*

Smaller than a sparrow
and ten times as fast,
the green humming bird is,
then isn't.

❋

The shepherd reads his own hands
in the lee of the rock.
Only his dog enters the wind
to check my approach.

❋

Late night writing,
a beetle on my glaring page.
The lights of the next mountain's village –
stars at the foot of our bed.

At Cementerio De La Recoleta

A suburb of the richly dead,
their coffins stacked like suitcases
in the holds of black marble ships.
These names still demand
too much attention.

Beyond the Doric gate
the city mirrors the polished tombs;
collectors of cardboard push
their barrows through the streets,
trudging with worn-out shoes,
while slick-haired men fete
their mistresses in restaurants.

It's spring in Buenos Aires:
the young are music in the park
and there's the scent of white cedar trees
for those who still have time.

The Goldberg Variations

(for Víkingur Ólaffson)

The imagined scene:
late, the fire crackles low.
Count Keyserlingk, sleepless,
turns in his bed, racked by gout.
In an adjoining room the Goldberg boy
plays softly, lightly, crystalline harpsichord –

something bright and cheerful,
gentle to the small-houred soul
and its circular reflections.
Something to feel not so alone
in this life, the passing of it, as in the decay
of the clavier's last note.

Refreshed again by new-fingered invention,
this is no music to sleep to
(we were never going to sleep)
and by the fifth variation it seems
we are running through a forest
pursued by a bear.

In the slow Canone we walk together
through the dreaming town, silent
except for our footsteps crunching snow.
Not a door open,
not one candle in a window
and the bells, between strikes.

Variation seventeen, we rise over the roofs
of Dresden, chimney pots stilled of smoke,
the stars bright with cold. We fly
like archangels, our fur coats
streaming behind us.
Ursa Major is ours, the Pole Star, the Plough.

What is the bird that sings in twenty-eight,
long before the sun?
Not an owl's lonely questioning – how, how?
The Nachtigall perhaps?
Then in the Quodlibet, distant folk songs,
an old ornate clock, ticking, loud.

All the while, Prussia defeats Austria,
Celsius invents his scale,
Bering sails from Russia and the Dutch poor
cry out for bread. Count Keyserlingk, ambassador,
would like to leave this world, his world, behind
and float again on that Aria.

Johann Gotlieb Goldberg
teenager, 'note eater', plays by sight
Bach's shifting patterns of stillness,
his sureness and surprise
arrivals and departures
in the restless inner night.

From

Invisible Mending

2016

Adelaide

You old quincunx.
Colonel Light playing tic tac toe
on the Kaurna's pages,
that little brownsnake of a river
winding through its parklands frame.

Over your eastern stairs the sun appears,
filtering through skylights,
the footfall echo of your arcades,
to end with a long bath in the west –
your curve of beaches
which are summer's collective.

Clever, pretty, but lacking confidence,
exposed here on your plain.
We always have to talk you up,
get your festival clothes on.

I like you best in November
when you spill buckets of jacaranda,
April too, when the slow light cools
into shouts in the stadia.
Even now, after a week of 40 degrees –
it's raining at last,
upstairs at the Exeter I can hear
chuckles in the gutters
and applause from the rooftops.
Beyond the brown haze of your suburbs
we smell desert,
so we love to see the water run.

Adelaide – *heimat* of sandstone Terraces,
gargoyles, lacunae, suffocations.
Once I thought you were too small,
but after all these years we fit each other:
here in front of Bonython Hall,
my first memory – a pantomime giant
came down through the floodlit trees
chasing Jack and his golden harp.

Place is voice as much as view:
'Legs like Payneham Road.'
'A pash at Windy Point' –
It's better up there than Los Angeles,
that hot glitter, all the way to the Gulf.

Learn to Speak the Language

I was on the bus to town.
On the seat in front of me
two women were chatting in Punjabi,
and the guy sitting next to me says:
'If you come to this country
you should learn to speak the language.'

'Yeah. You're right,' I said,
'So how's your Kaurna?
And how good are ya
at Pitjantjatjara?
Fancy a chat in Ngarkat?

And you know, it's a pity we don't hear
more Peramangk at the bank,
more Tiwi on the TV,
more Wik at the picnic
and Arrernte on the verandah.

And, if you expect to live here,
you really oughta
know some Yorta Yorta,
get your tongue
around Bundjalung,
grasp the meaning in Mirning
and know the score
in Eora.

Kamilaroi and Wiradjuri,
Luritja and Warlpiri,
understand their poetry.

You're right, if you come to this country,
You should learn to speak the language.'

Bedroom Ceiling Fan

White medusa
above our reef,
we watch its life cycle
a fathom down.

In summer it never sleeps,
moving the night's hot breath
on pale, cruciform bodies,
minds refusing to close.

In winter
it lies still,
a three-petalled flower of ice.

It is the turning reel
of our private cinema,
projecting onto these sheets
the amateur porn
of positions we've tried.

Fever sweats,
loneliness,
laughter.

A boring film
where the characters
read books by bedside lights,
and neither speaks.

Times we lie apart in anger,
far as the edges of the bed allow.
Wasted nights.

Here, your waters break twice:
underground springs
no muscle can stop.

Baby heads grow in the white field,
breathing milk,
howling the slow incision of teeth.
The buddhas become long and bony,
flop down between us
wanting to know what to do with their lives –
as we pretend to know.

My black curly hair
greys and shrinks
to a widow's peak.
Your long chestnut waves
are cropped and dyed.

We are buried in the rustle of weekend papers,
their slightly-altered, repeating stories:
the greedy privatise gain and socialise loss,
husbands and wives cheat each other, leaders their states,
the so-very-reasonable sell guns to fanatical haters,
people destroy what exists, believing in what doesn't –
and we live in the hegemony of gloss.

On setting one, it is a whisper,
a rumour, a silk dressing gown undone.

On setting two, sweet breezes start to blow.

On setting three, it knocks a rhythm
like the lovers climaxing below.

On setting four, it is a white beehive,
an inner sea, a shallow roar.

On setting five, it is a cyclone's light-bulb eye.

Slow down now, slow down, slow.

Reveg

This sheep station has
a concentration-camp haircut;

on the stony hill
replanted Callitris
forms
              a patchy fuzz.

We are growing

two hundred years
of our madness

out.

Travelling the Golden Highway, Thinking of Global Warming

Stringybarks in bloom;
a perfume like honey ice cream.

Along the Prussian blue escarpment
two eagles work the updraft.

Cicada noise rises and falls
as if the mountain itself was breathing –

In panic.   Out relax.
In panic.   Out relax.

Manga pylons stride the valley,
millions of volts in their fists –

The car radio is plunged into static,
silver grids of capital/energy shift –

Open cuts. Artificial mesas –
Ulan coal warms the world.

Black Swans Mating

At first she is a lone writer
reaching down into the taupe
of the lake.

Feeling for weed-words,
a ribbon of sentence.

Finding a morsel,
she pushes it under herself,
building a book,
a raft for her species.

That black snake of a neck
tipped with red
is constantly scribbling.

Then he arrives, swan-sails in.

She launches
from her self-created island
to glide and moor beside him.

But first the dance.

Chests thumping the water,
beaks dipping,
necks cross-ways and up and back.

And yes, there are times
when in symmetry
they form the outline
of a ruffled heart in black.

He fast treads water
and lifts onto her,
wings thrown back and beating.

At the peak
they honk and almost squeal
then straighten their necks to the sky.

And who is to say
they don't feel ecstasy,
satisfied lovers
knowing their lover
satisfied as well?

The Cicada Quartets

The cicada plays a guiro,
a wooden scraper
in the throat
of summer.

The cicadas place
their Geiger counters
among the trees.
This must be a lethal dose.

Trapped, the cicada stutters
against the ceiling.
Once, he filled the whole stadium
with his voice.

Cicadas, all day you built
the wall of heat.
Now the thunder has silenced you,
and the rain, ozone sweet.

Cicada, your dried carapace
like pharaoh's winding sheet.
A hollow, full of the
memory of sound.

My Father at the Clothesline.

Concentrating on each peg, mouth open,
aghast at the rate the world is leaving him.
His dignity, as he folds his clothes.

A Book of Hours at Rimbun Dahan

The light comes so slowly.
Another hazy, smoky dawn.
Dreams of my dead father woke me early.
There's too much time, then there's none.

❋

I start the great four-bladed ceiling fan.
Seconds later, a gecko drops to the floor,
stunned. Yes, the world's like that.
We all hang on as long as we can.

❋

In the house of shutters, but no window glass,
the outside world slips across dark-wood mirrors.
Shum hammering in the heat, Siti sweeping the path.
Life in slivers.

❋

Landing next to her, the little male dove
bobs so vehemently on the twig, it snaps.
His need to impress his love
means now they both must flap.

❋

Last night a gecko ate a grasshopper's body
but left its head, still alive this morning, on the floor.
Time eats you like that, but more slowly.
You become a twitching mask of thoughts.

*

Mosquitoes fly out when you shift something black,
whining and hiding again in the room.
Some people I know like to hurry back
to restore themselves in comfortable gloom.

*

That cicada sounds like a dentist,
drilling all day into my eye-tooth nerve.
Shrilling on and on about Time,
everything I love, but can't preserve.

*

The swallows loop back over the pond,
dive and circle, as they must do.
Words repeat in my mind; words
I failed to say when I most needed to.

*

Gathering thunder. The eye of the day
winks smoky orange, slips under
a tuduk of purple and monsoon grey.
Add to this drama, the bilal and rooster.

*

Out of the sky of luminous black
rain falls joyfully. You and I
who lived so long alone together
now walk again under one umbrella.

*

The lotus leaves hold silver discs,
small worlds of water above the pond.
Why did I think my circle so small
and nothing beyond?

*

The wren in the dripping congea vine
flutters off water from the storm.
Our ceiling leaked; on the floor puddles shine.
Resilient, in the after-light, the quiet forms.

*

The sour smoke of roadside fires,
rubbish smoulders at end of day.
Old needs, hopes half-realised,
and something else we threw away.

*

The pattern of the stone path disappears
under a new green ikat of moss.
Walking it gives me a change of mood.
Why all this thinking about loss?

*

Under the mosquito net, settling to sleep,
you feel safe from the world's attacks.
Then you hear the needling, invisible whine
of that one mosquito inside the net; the mind.

*

From the estate's wall, grey macaques leap
into the laden mango tree.
From your side of the bed, you told me to sleep,
but the night's so warm, and I want something juicy.

Gasoline Flowers

Mohamed Bouazizi,
wanting living space
and a little justice,
became an orange-yellow orchid

Thich Quang Duc,
a wavering lotus of flame

Palden Choetso – a smoky iris,
deadly bright at its centre.

For his land of snow
and a spinning prayer,
Tsering Tashi was a gaping petro hibiscus.

The Museum of Memory, Santiago de Chile

(for Raul Zurita and Juan Garrido-Salgado)

The Mapocho hurries to the sea

there is electricity in the iron bed

the snow smells like polished metal

100,000 students are on the streets

the howl that came out of me did not sound human

the shantytown's tree turns white

I was bleeding from my nipples

the students' hair is wet with snow

the river is really just a mountain stream

120 V

< >

240 V

and from my vagina

Neruda died then

the umbrella vendors arrive with the snow

do you ever want to see your children again?

the faces of the student leaders on television

- 1.5

- 1 - 2

.5 - 2.5

AMPERES

the river is always in a hurry

do you ever want to sleep with your wife again?

they have learnt not to trust the cameras

his breathing became more and more hoarse

GENERAL ELECTRIC

the march was peaceful

there was nothing on the world news

the snow smells clean

the river hurries

the bed is wired

From

Transit

2007

Camping Ground Desiderata

Watch sorties of ravens and magpies
as you sip your beer, cooled on ice.
It was a long drive here,
looking for silence and birdsong.

Note how the stony path
holds the range in miniature,
and come to savvy
the strata of things.

See beyond the workday pixels
glows a hill of spinifex
and another
and another.

Hurry with the going of the light
and rise with the rising of it,
feeling patterns of convection,
gully winds at dawn and dusk.

Name the stars
with a hopelessly distant love,
point out shapes
to your children.

Observe even the smallest wren
pegs out its territory.
Feel again a tangible economy
of shelter, fire and food.

Be intimate once more with the dirt:
in your plate, in your hair,
in the loop roads of your guts.
The grime under your nails telling where
we came from and where we go.

Of the South

Frugal land.
Home of mallee and olive and grape.
Slow life, slow growth,
rare big timbers.
Square-cut institutes,
old schools, the parish mind;
stone architecture enters the voices.

Landscape that won't flaunt itself –
a spring in the hillside's lee,
an underground cave,
a secret beach,
salty pinks of inter-dune lakes.

Everything lonely and waiting,
or resigned to little –
friends who think of each other
but haven't met for years;
a visit would be extravagant.

I look down and find my hands
have begun to wrinkle
on the pages of poetry books.
I can see myself become
an old stubborn tree of the South.

Kayaking

(for Patricia Irvine)

The day is green,
the light at the edge of clouds
sobering the river.
Mangrove blossom
scents the air with a bouquet
like the bottom of a fruit crate –
something tropical, yet wood-slat.

Sleek and lustrous and slimy grey,
a mother dolphin and her calf
farm the shallows,
backs arching down and again down,
driving glimmers of silver
from Port River weed.

Swan Alley, Shooting Creek,
The Cutting: our kayaks
slap the chop or glide into shush
to hear the invisible wren,
the loping croaks of white-faced heron.

Emerging from reflected acres of leaf
to where the powerlines hum,
we approach industrial heaven:
sculptural wrecks, gantries, derricks,
the hooded brontosaurial rust –
Jonahs inside the ribs of echoing whales.

Around the point, the wind turns
and we work to a more-distant shore,
pushing in rhythm, like gangers or lovers.
A pair of sharp-tailed sandpipers
startles from the bank –
Autumn is coming
and all the miles to Siberia.

Junior Football

I like to watch the primary colours clash
and hear the caws beside the boundary line,
the *round the necks!* and *in the backs!*
I like the hawks and bulls and lions
on homemade banners flapping in the wind –
the team 'runners' with arthritic hips,
the car horns from the hill that greet a goal,
collective groans that echo round a miss.
Sweet oranges that grin from plastic buckets,
clouds of liniment in tatty changing rooms,
the smell of mud and grass between the sprigs
that clatter onto concrete like sudden hail.
Half time: aunts and uncles tong the barbie.
I like the hiss and then sometimes the taste
of sausages spitting their social grease.
Coaches: circled by the teams, philosophic,
or ranting bitter losers who swear at kids.
Umpires: just older than the under fourteens,
or pushing fifty, a kick or two behind the game,
inventing which way to give the frees.
The beer-holding, fag-smoking parents
overweight in Saturday's tracky daks
cheer their progeny surging down the wings.
The rumble of the boots like horses' hooves,
the thump and tumble of the ball –
this high ritual, that lifts suburban roofs.

Relief Teacher

Bespectacled, tall,
voice high and thin.
Dome spattered with age,
a too-hopeful grin.

In maths
he tried to tell
parables of gardens.
We gave him hell.

The division of plants,
how fruits multiply seeds,
curves of leaf and flower,
all the symmetries.

Our jeering so loud
the headmaster burst in,
led the old man away,
the last we saw of him.

Among thousands of lessons
his I recall, one of a few.
Sixty years too late,
give him his due.

Last Thoughts of a Famous Dog

In his grey coat, he seemed a friendly man,
leaning towards me with a piece of meat.
I followed, jumped into his van –
the last I saw of my Moscow street.

We drove through suburbs I didn't know,
I snuffled and scratched at the bars.
Those first flakes of Autumn snow
hit the windscreen and drifted off like stars.

A uniformed man lifted the boom,
we passed through the gates of an institute.
Washed and fed, kept in a sterile room,
I was named and numbered – a new recruit.

I remember a dark journey in another van
down roads that never seemed to end.
I sniffed the frozen air of Kazakhstan,
and scented something burnt in the wind.

From my porthole I see the sky's arc expand,
below me, the vanishing cosmodrome.
Noise and killing heat. Now I understand –
this famous dog is never coming home.

Housing Estate in the Howard Era

Modular mansions in pastels and creams,
'Entertainment areas' designed
around wide-screen TVs.
The windows are huge
but the curtains are drawn –
Pragmatism won't see it is ideology.

Fat-arsed cars are the local gods,
and double garages their shrines.
Gardens shrunk to lozenges and tabs,
and narrow paths to the washing lines.
More bedrooms than people.
These structures agree:
'Don't relate to the street.
Everything's inside, and for me.'

Cliché

You're a cocktail, a heady one –
if accidental: tragic,
if opportune: golden,
dressed in khaki: instantly heroic.
Up all night on TV,
by dawn, you're rosy.
Down memory lane
you can't walk, but trip –
though when you fall
you always land on your feet.
Democratically elected,
you're the Minister For Truth,
but if there's more to the story
it won't meet the eye.
Your name is household,
your face an icon,
your history a legend,
and your ending is happy,
sealed with a kiss.

The Peregrine

He's back again, the peregrine:
I can hear him, but not see.
He must be standing
on the high-frequency wires
atop this edifice
like the plain truth of geometry
and his querulous '*reap-reap*'
haunts the conditioned office.

Sometimes I look over the computer screen
through the oblongs of glass
that are all sky
and the aftermath drifts down;
pigeon breast feathers
and longer ones from the outer wing
and I know the peregrine
is going about his work.

It's hard, to be caught between
the miracle of existing at all
and no longer being,
and though I dream I'm falcon
I know I'm pigeon,
tapping my days by the ledge
until the '*reap-reap*'
and the claws of the peregrine.

In Praise of the Colour Grey

The fur of night animals –
powdery, speckled, moon strays.

Dull birds with glorious songs.
Blue Whales, mostly grey.

Clouds crossing the depths of wells.
The first and last of the day.

The photos of Cotton and Strand,
their daisies and subways.

Promises of fog-bound cities,
the shine of unwritten slate.

In this age of new rigidities
I praise the colour grey,

emblem of fields uncertain –
it might go either way.

Bat in a Pantry

You're home at last from the night shift,
hanging from the handle of the coffee grinder
by your micro grapple-hook feet.

If only those humans wouldn't flit in and out,
clicking that annoying little sun,
and must they make so much noise?

Your ears minutely swivel, even in your sleep.
Rich fur is bunched about your neck –
'bald mouse' how dare they call you that!

You are a beautiful baby buggy,
leather hood folded down,
struts fine-boned for the sky.

When darkness eases in,
you will leave this cardamom-heavy air
and fly against the lacework of the stars

into the webbed dreams
of pantry keepers,
tossing, flightless, on their beds.

From

Rooms and Sequences

2003

From *Anakhronismos*

3

Today I'm thinking of Busarius,
just nineteen, recruited from Liguria,
his mother a famous singer
and he rising rapidly for his years.
Last month he drove to a quarry in the hills
and shot himself.
There were no hints;
he appeared happy in his work,
though now I think of it
his laughter always seemed
a little too high and loud.
The funeral was wretched –
his mother full of drink and pills,
no one knowing what to say.
And now, having never paid him
due attention in his life,
I notice Busarius everywhere:
in markets, at the hippodrome,
glimpsing his likeness in public urinals,
hearing that high girlish laugh
in every feasting crowd.

9

Maximus took me for a spin
in his new ultra-light.
Flying low into the eastern sun,
we followed our one spidery river,
barely a trickle this summer.

Too many aqueducts drawing it off
to grow these orchards out of dust.
One either side,
just a few leagues distant,
the land's blank parchment.

Our lifeline is choked
down to one small thread.
No wonder the temples here
belong to the Eumenides –
the fates at which we don't
(if we can help it) look.

11

I saw them washed up in their raft –
the Parthians, ragged, half-dead from the sea.

No one could imagine their journey.
Why land here with their women and children?

Orders from Rome:

abandon them in the desert,
or drag them back out to sea.

15

Adonis lays tiles.
Dressed only in shorts,
he walks to his van
parked in the side street.

You can see all the muscles
in his wide shoulders
and supple back,
his long, lightly haired legs.
All the girls turn to watch –
think of his hard brown body
stretched out on the cool tiles.

20

Yesterday in the Colonnades
I heard Parapus, that sickening orator,
thumping the lectern
with his favourite word –
'Sacred!' 'Sacred!'

Some terms are dangerous.
They're kept in government safehouses,
killed or unleashed
at moments of crisis.

I'll tell you what's 'sacred' to me –
the look I saw on a young woman's face
(she'd been pacing the cavern
of the Central Railway Station)
the look on her face when her lover
finally arrived.

34

I used to keep everything,
every scrap of a mention,
each little peep of my name.
Now I throw it all away.
No one will go through my archives
wanting to know who I was.

This life is no more
than a day by the sea:
you come, you go,
the beach remains.

From *Ninety-One Hotel Rooms*

The walls have ears, yes, but
If only they had tongues:
what would seep out
from these wallpaperings
of houndstooth and paisley,
these flowers that never were?
Fights of young lovers
on their first overseas trips.
Crims hiding out in one-star hotels
speaking lines from no-star movies.
Lonely dreams, nightmares of work,
all those long-distance calls.
Ecstatic fucking words rumpling white sheets,
the silky frictive voice of all our skins.

A Vegetative Life

Beetroot

Cutting you
is pitchforking earth in Silesia.

Under your skin
sombre as last season's nest
lies radical magenta.

Thinking a bright, steaming borscht,
I work in the mud
and the pelting rain.

Asparagus

I smell cut grass –
which is exactly
what you are,
but thicker, more primitive.

Laid on white bread:
green penises draped
in cotton.
The excitement is
in the tip.

Potato

The landlords averted their eyes
when you came up rotten,

collapsed to stinky pulp
in their tenants' fists.

Heavy, solid, a river stone,
now cool and white in my hand –
the newborn smell of spud.

You scattered a generation,
planting Galways and Dublins
in the New World.

Parsnip

You will do
for a witch's nose
or a reverend's
Sunday roast.
Your name is parsimonious
prim and clipped
at the end.
You look so straight
but the devil's in you –
parsnip wine
is the strongest brew
I've ever tasted,
sending the mind
through burning hoops.
Pale digits of the damned,
you go into the fire
and come out saved.

Red Onion

Medieval model of the spheres,
gyroscope by Fabergé,
you contain infinity –
and make me weep.

The Sturt Highway

Now the last light catches old fridges resurrected as mailboxes on the plain –

a voice says 'I AM' from a burning roly-poly bush

there: a little mound some farmer bulldozed just to break the horizontal

Kenworths and Macks in their prides
roaring down the gears through the drowse of distant towns

the road/house conjunction:
road lifted and folded into walls, the spatter of fluoro lights

an insect never before seen,
green phosphorescent head, intricate lace wings & ruby eyes,
peels from the windscreen

a white moon with the sky to itself
a crow on a roadside marker

Three Studies of a Rotary Hoist

Far off a plane is tuning the sky.
The blue becomes white-hot.
Looking up through triangulations
and parallelograms of wire
think detention centres. Bright
plastic pegs, burrs on razor wire.
Absent people, hung out to dry.
In this design, the empty, weight
bearing arms of a desert power pyramid
oppress the quotidian base.
Down the road, a mower whines
on and on like the prime minister,
and the hoist doesn't catch fire.

Astrolabe on a deck of lawn,
taking the azimuth of Orion's head
or a corner bearing on Antares.
Stuck here together,
we're sailing just through time.
Pegging out these soggy ghosts
that will be rinsed again in dew,
I feel a spider brush my hand
with his soft structural engineering.
The wind rises, soughing
the trees in my neighbour's yard;
that big house which never filled with children.
A cricket sounds like a pressed-tin toy
and the hoist keens, its metal voice, deeply felt.
Waving flags at what horizon?

Concentric circles of white,
my mother (arms up) in the centre.
Whey pillowcases whirled high
against the front of light.
Stranded wires of nostalgia
like the wavy green of a two-dollar note,
glowing kero heaters, and milk in bottles.
I lobbed a threepenny bunger into my father's
Y-fronts, pegged and baggy
and blew the arse out in a smouldering circle.
'*What a fart!*' we joked, two simian boys
riding on the arms of the Adelaide–Sydney model,
making the hoist groan and skirl.
Or hand over hand moving through the wires,
the marks left on our fingers like 'the cuts'.
Jawbreaker or chinwhacker, the solid handle
seized up now at the bottom of the yard.

The Daylight Owl

And yesterday the bird of night did sit,
Even at noon-day, upon the market place

1.

All day the alarm system
of musk lorikeets
stuck on 'intruder'.
Sorties of miners and fatter
stealth bombers –
warnings, warnings, warnings,
a demented chatter
harsh as police radio.

The daylight owl,
still in his otherness,
silent in his wrong,
only blinks.
Shifts one craggy claw
on the bough,
weathers
this garish abuse.

Eventually, even the well-seasoned
have enough of hate
and he flies into the dusk,
distress beacons fading down.

2.

Like retrospective tax –
what went wrong that year
we could blame on the owl?
In the winter I suffered a nervous collapse.
Doing a sudden somersault on ice,
my wife broke her back.
But there were also good things,
a year like a sine wave, in fact.

I used to believe in omens
and other games of the mind;
ten years old,
if I couldn't run to the top of the drive
before the next car passed, I'd die.

But let's not get mythic.
So many things, in time,
will prove at least half right.
The owl was just an owl,
caught in the glaring prose
of daylight.

Murray Bend

Easy as a grebe skims the overflow
then settles to the lapwing's cry,
those samphire colours warm the eye.
Paint this glow if you can, or turn
to the speckles of light, that main-channel glitter
there, under the willows where old caravans lie
and surplus train carriages come to rest.
The galvo collage of those river-stepped shacks:
Bonnie Doon, Kooringal, and *Jindabyne* –
their sculptural tanks, and cubist sides.
Sun-warmed tar on the planks
above the splash of cloudy green.
Rusted pump country, big fish dreaming place.

Parawa Farmer

After fifty years the shambling cows have turned his hills
into long-line verse.

Stanza by half-rhymed stanza, he reads their terraced paths –
the same trudging theme.

The farmhouse is set among stringybarks and gloomy pine,
damp even in summer,

in winter, a messy tomb, habitable in dim circles between
fire, stove, and bed.

His dog follows him, one kick behind. Only television visits.
They listen to the rain.

In the morning, the farmer splashes his face with ache water,
fingers his wrinkled skin.

A raven, black as any sump, flies out of the glittering trees,
calling his name.

Prayer

A pincer movement of rain clouds –
we're outflanked in the gassy light
driving through these mid-North towns
which cling to life
the way the topsoil clings
just above the shale.

Boys of milk-white stone
bend over their rifles
to inspect the poppies,
plastic, tubercular red,
in crosses at their feet.
The same face in every town,
as though they were brothers.

The car moves into the Willochra plain,
the Southern Flinders like Gallipoli
but with a more ancient sea.
My children's faces reflect in dust-streaked windows.

May you never crawl or lie
in the stinking charnel
that is the basement
of all empires.

May you run up stony hills
only to picnic or make love.

May you never carry a pack
heavy with death-fear or death-wish.

This said silently
to a rear-view mirror.

When we arrive
it's already night.
The sheds where the volunteers came from
grey, looming polygons,
silent of sheep –
a farm only for tourists.
Behind us, the black range,
then stars, what stars –
Rigel (falling)   Sirius (falling)

A cold, autumn moon
shining on the blind eyes
of the boy soldiers,
back there,
guarding the sleeping towns.

Letter Found in a Vacant Lot

Dear Peter, how are you keeping?
ripgut, burdock, and shards of wood
Long time since we've heard from you
just a pit where the cellar was
Say a mass for Betty who died last May
a fence, and a letterbox, all that's left
a hell of a job and you can't find anything
a new shoot where the lemon tree stood
having radio therapy for 'C'
some broken bricks in the skeleton weed
still it goes ok and doesn't use any oil
magpies drinking from a muddy pool
all fairly well but the little'uns miss
junk mail mostly, letters from the church
Write soon, we haven't heard for years

Spinal Unit

Burn is an old metaphor for pain,
but I think *spine* should also qualify
as I walk long corridors to the sign:
Burns Unit this way, *Spinal* that,
then take the red arrow to the right.

The beds are altars decked with flowers.
I place her poppies in the last natural light –
watching each of the patients
brace for their separate nights.
In the shadows sits an old fat god –
I pray soft-soled Morphine brings them sleep.

In a saline drip, a flood in the upper chamber
hardly moves the bottom flow –
how do you know another's pain?
I hear her words and stroke her hand
but just surmise. Her backbone,
below that sweet skin, an unguessed reef.

If she could turn her head, I would show her
in the gardens darkening below
an escaped balloon is drifting.
It follows where the evening breeze blows –
uncertain and so bright
in the long shadows of the trees.

This is as much as I can describe.

About Your Poem . . .

Your poem was too soft,
we couldn't get to sleep on it
no matter which way we turned.
Your poem was completely transparent
when wet.
The congregation was shocked.
At the crucial moment it jammed
and the wheels fell off.

It was too shiny, too fat
and far too red.
It didn't go with the curtains.
At a modest depth
it stopped ticking altogether.

Your poem was unsafe for infants,
with those small plastic parts.
It refused to use its litter tray
and stank up our home.

Your poem was a bit too dainty,
couldn't reach the revs or take the torque.
Its ratings were low
in the 25-40 demographic.
Furthermore,
it chafed us around the crotch.

As much as we like your poem
we are returning it –
the only person it fits, is you.

From

Close to Home

2000

Domestic Mystery #1

A portable hunger
dragging itself from room to room –

Its belly split open,
we peer in to read
oracles of dust:

sewing pins,
a swirly blue marble
like a little Earth,

and that crucial piece
of the puzzle –
the edge of the chalet
where it touches the sky.

Droning sadly like age,
a thin whine
sucking on thinning carpets,

it shifts pitch upwards
to complain
when cornered or blocked.

In its heart
its reason to exist:
that nature abhors it.

Domestic Mystery #2

Great eye of forgetfulness,
unblinking anaesthetist –
you could lose twenty years
in front of this thing
and hardly know.

Teak veneer or fascist plastic black –
lacking the warmth of our own stories
but full of the cold crackle
of corporate dreaming,
the global flickers
of youth, beauty and style.

One of my worst fears
it'll be on loud in the ward where I'll die –
the last image in my mind
a Lucille Ball wail, colour saturated,
sucking me down into the eternal Re-run
somewhere between stations.

And yet, a certain cosiness –
isobars unthreatening on the box,
slippers, a beer, and the late-night movie.
The summer sleeping spell of a million runs,
a thousand tumbling wickets,
and the comfort of feeding our children
the same images we fed upon.

Articulately dumb, violently bland,
above all, everywhere – mud hut to condo.
Ninety-nine channels,
everything/nothing to watch.

Vasectomy

He said '*lie back,*
look out the window'
while he snipped,
and then (I swear it!)
chatted golf –
his slice/the splice
and tapping the balls in.

Out the window was only sky,
a loose bit of gutter
flapping in the breeze –
'budget cuts'
was all I thought.

Afterwards he sprayed this stuff
worse than fire,
but I got up glad –
a triumph over nature,
the human will
and all that guff.

Still glad next day
though the sack swelled up
apple sized, purple, a witch's fruit –
I practised a spell,
'*no more rubber, no more pills,*
no more rubber, no more pills.'

Then bad dreams all week –
trains smashing through the kids
as they sat in our yellow Ford,
big trucks that kept on coming,
me left on cliff tops
with empty arms.

Poem for Two Brickies

Iambic below,
from stack to flick –
soft strong/ soft strong/ soft strong.

The mirrored trochee stands above,
strong soft/ strong soft/ strong soft –
catch to second stack.

Between the two,
the material
made weightless –
caesurae of an afternoon.

From clothbound hand
to clothbound hand –
each earth-fired book
placed to wait
on its invisible shelf of air.

Natural History #6

Potatoes breathe easiest under a full moon.
Scallops dance at high tide, even in hotel kitchens.
Elephants tread so very carefully,
listening for the slightest tremor of the Earth.
A cockroach will live nine days without its head.
Crocodiles cannot poke out their tongues.
A snail can sleep for three years
and all polar bears are left-handed.
Abbreviation is a longish word,
nothing much rhymes with *poetry*,
and are question marks OK?
On the first day of eternity my true love gave to me
the square root of minus one.

Mythology, a Rough Guide

White butterflies are messengers from heaven –
the news is not necessarily good.

A heron persuades some fish
that their pond will soon become dry,
offering to carry them to new and better lakes –
you guess the rest.

Good things to own:
the arrow that returns after hitting its target,
the bag that remains full of food,
the shirt that enables you to fly.

Those who are rescued
sometimes turn and devour their rescuers,
so don't assume too much gratitude.

The small and weak but clever
can defeat the big and strong but stupid.
The big, strong and clever, are however, a problem.

Don't forget that a king may well have the head of a pig.

A lovely woman met in a dream can be encountered the next day –
often wearing a large snake around her neck.

A nymph from heaven who loses the least little scarf
can never return, so please check your belongings before you depart.

Power Cut

Carefully, at the dispenser,
I make a cup of tea,
filling it up by sound.

In a square of daylight,
I watch my breath
sigh over the cup.

Four storeys down
car tyres on the road,
a wet rhythm, flanging up.

Lightning –
people caught on the median strip
automatically duck –

I see one bolt
strike a crane arm,
the brilliant geometry of Zig.

When the lights come back,
the computer screens
are locked on 'WAIT',

as if a God logged in,
gently kissed them,
told them how to find peace.

From the stairwell
the sound of tourists
in a sudden cathedral.

The Key

I looked for the key
in many kinds of water;
bright creeks with sandstone floors,
dark, ferry-churned harbours.

I looked for the key
in bookshops on rainy days,
in a whispering forest of stringybarks,
in all sorts of bottles.

I looked for the key
in museums and in cello cases.
I looked desperately between rocks
on a barren Greek island.

I thought the key would be bronze,
covered in ancient characters.
I always pictured myself
holding it in both hands.

Then I wondered if the key
mightn't be the little silver one
dangling from my daughter's bracelet –
or maybe not key-shaped at all.

Perhaps a certain set of notes
whistled on a chilly, starry night.
A phrase, whispered into the right ear
opening everything –

Shower with My Son

We shower together –
I hold up your small slippery body
to the laughing spray.

You uncircumcised,
me circumcised –
when I was your age
it was the fashion
to cut off a bit –

I wonder how long I screamed?
I wonder what sort of world
I thought I was dealing with?

You are so centred
in that compact, muscly body
like a civet, or a cub.

Me, I live too much in my head
which I'd love to turn off for a while –

just feel the world through muscle,
understand it with the eye.

Children's Hospital

Suddenly my son's a passenger.
Beyond the portholes of The Great Ship
lies our own (now foreign) country.
We have to learn new ropes;
instructions on the wall convey 'the procedure for fluids',
in his folder there's 'The Glasgow Coma Line'.
These charts don't show the moon,
but pupil sizes from one to five.

The clocks are wrong or missing.
Look up, and it's dark again.
Over the great bulkhead Orion circles,
and car lights stream down the hill in a long white wake.

All its decks blazing with light,
The Great Ship ploughs on through our sleep
and little seabirds cry in the night.

Coda

My father's father thrashed his son
with a razor strop,
not only for what he knew he'd done –
'This is for what I didn't see!'
he'd say, dealing out another one
or three – grandma hysterical
when the boy passed out.

My father's father had shiny shoes,
sold Winning Post chocolates
all through the Great Depression.

But there's a coda to this –
things seen in a fuller light.
Back in the fifties,
when my father sprang into the sky
at centre-half-forward for The Blues,
his father insisted on
shining his boots.

Did it lovingly, every weekend.

2,4,6,8

Blue-jowled, tight-wired,
mean mouth and hard hand,
Mr B was not a good teacher.
His lessons rambling, confused,
often ended with an explosion
in some kid's puffy face,
legs yardsticked,
or other casual bashings.

One day he broke completely.
The class came in after lunch,
found him head down at his desk,
crying into folded arms.
'My dad wouldn't've let you get away with that.
My dad wouldn't've let you get away with that.'
Over and over, till the head was fetched.

Mr B finished up in the library,
banging books back in steel shelves,
his cruel hand neat on overdue slips.
Only one of his teachings stays with me
(beside the clear, violent lesson
of what a bad father can do to a son)
it's this one: *2,4,6,8.*
He said it suddenly, loudly, one afternoon,
interrupting himself and stopping the class dead –
'The date is the second of April, 1968!
Don't you realise, none of us
will ever see a day like it again!'

Gathering

Drag out blue irises
and lines by Tennyson –
the only one that really fits:
'We know nothing.'

When they call for a minute's
silence
there's always
some chicken truck roaring past,
or a trench digger at work
in the south-west corner.

The infants are restless
and kick against their prams.
Behind them, in wheelchairs,
the octogenarians survey
their own future crowd:
the brave, the clever, the mute, the small.

The funeral director warms to her theme –
a slightly amplified and tinny
'it comes to us all.'

Beside another bed,
a woman in a white hat
bends to sniff a rose.

Waiting Room, Bundanoon Station

'*Shane luvs Jade*', perhaps it's still true,
scribbled all those years ago
on the waiting-room wall, duck-egg blue.
It would be cold here in winter, a sparrow

might hunker to its nest (tucked in there
below the joist) and a man strike a match
just to cup his hands around the flare.
A bell rings. The signal swings down like a latch.

'Rabbit, Sparrow and Bucko wuz ere.'
But where are they now? And '*Gail*'?
In bushland last year
some remains were found near a fire trail.

Think of her standing in this room,
scratching her name with a twenty-cent bit –
running from doom
straight into it.

The two fifteen rounds the curve,
its headlight shining like a second sun.
The station master comes out to observe
a couple of stragglers start to run.

Flatland

(for John Griffin)

Living in this flat land (insects on a mirror)
we can never get very far from ourselves.

The River Light winds through Lower Light and is just that –
a stream of rock, and donkey-coloured illuminations.

Surrounded by bleating stones,
there's a place here called Dublin where no Liffey runs

then further on, at the proving range,
all things may fly in clear parabolas.

Crushed by massive sky,
our beings are smaller than we hoped –

we have to imagine mountains
any higher than the salt farm's mocking range.

A man (visible for miles) burns off autumn grass,
like some damned prophet on the plain.

Pools

1. Motel Pool

The storm bird
calls from the bushes
behind the motel pool –

it elongates moments,
heavies sky,
humidifies the mind.

In the pool,
the tourist children fight.
All around, the suburbs spread –

and the storm bird
repeats itself.

2. Shallow Stream

In sweet, shallow Belongil,
tea-coloured,
I lie facing the sky.

Water courses blood-warm
over my eardrums,
soft as air current's feathery trickle.

Eyes shut, I think back on my life
and come up with (pleasantly)
nothing.

Voices with the treble turned off –
my daughter, my wife, her mother,
three generations of women looking down on me,
as if into a grave.

3. The Falls

The girls,
golden like frogs,
breaststroke across the pool
to the falls.

A hard, cold shower
awaits them on the other shore
where stones are slapped and kissed.

A chill breeze ripples the pool's skin
and light stars out
from its sun-plumbed murk.

Now the girls
warm themselves on angular rocks,
the ferns beside them
all a-shiver.

4. Waterslide

The pool under the water slide
is a space for blue exaltations –
the sloshing curves, the dips down
known for the first time.

And I join the shivery kids
climbing the dripping stairs,
excited that here at least
I can take the ride again.

Fishing Shacks

A shocking mismatch of colours,
a love of galvo,
these bachelor beach pads
say 'boys' club'
in the boofiest way,
sometimes edged
with shotgun warnings –
the skull and cross bones
on the cubby door.

A total lack of tizz or frill
or any plants,
and a stack of stubbies
beside the gutting table.
The kitchen's outside, a grill
propped over charcoal piles.

Homage to its own solitude,
the architecture of rough enough,
of cobble together, of Rafferty's rules –
it says, '*live, but don't care too much*
about yourself.'

You can't complain –
a fire, some gar you've pulled
out of the bay,
the last sun
over turquoise fibro.

Back Lanes

Applique of weathered tin and light-soaked stone,
overflow of fig, sultana vine and nectarine,
covert of the shadow birds, the flitting,
darting passerines. Dark, delicious, deep
as in summer the last three fingers of shiraz –
the stories at the back of things,
the unknown if, the winding as.

From

Picture's Edge

1994

Shackville Midwinter

A town occupied by wind,

telescopes poised in empty rooms,

sunlight Hopperesque.

Now the shacks belong
to magpies and wandering dogs,
the lanes to crowds of soursobs.

Wood smoke:
I'm not alone,

perhaps another poet

renting space
for lines like these.

The Seagulls of Goulburn

In the cold town
racked by semis
they are white stillness
on a winter's night.

In summer
they shriek
by the bandstand
commemorating
a bloated Empress.

How do they survive
so far from their namesake?

They are as strange here
as white history,
they are cunning
and rapacious –
annexing families,
mining food from picnic blankets.

A group of them is called
a colony.

They watch the land
with red-rimmed eyes.

Almond Tree in a Scrap Metal Yard

They call it 'the salient'
as it first appears
in the embryo – the heart,
the leaping place –
the accidental plume
of red,
or the white
in a scrap metal yard
of an almond tree in bloom.

Impromptu

He's got it into his head
that we never die
if we believe in a him
called the Lord –
I want to go outside,
at least he's given me
some mandarins.

Foraging in dark green,
the mock suns,
the mock moons,
mandarin picking.

In the grass below
I find a stunned thrush.
Was it the wires?
Was it the cold?

She closes her eyes.
It's no matter for moping this
but to be expected,
dramatised if you must
but look, the world is casual about it,
the sparrows keep chirping,
the mandarins have filled out
with winter rain.

Retreat

I've turned the TV up,
but I can't hear
the famous writer's words –
my child is squelching out
raw new vocabulary.

The writer's face
reflected in a train window
flashes through the countryside.
It's a nice shot.
She's pretending to compose
for the camera.

When the train arrives
a voice over says
'Change is painful.'
The baby rips the pen
out of my hand
saying 'My turn! My turn!'
and scribbles on this.

The camera glides up
to a big house by the sea,
the writer's retreat.
I give up,
crawl into a house
of upturned chairs,
a train of laughing pillows.

From

The Crack in the Crib

1984

The Bird Mother

Look through these windows –
she's working in the shed,
her face warmed by electric light.
Cold clearing night,
the ovary of the moon stuck in the bloodlines trees.
Only late in life abandoning
the Presbyterian past –
for her now religion has something to do
with infinite space and dust and ochre-red stars.
I see her spinning my veins out of her body,
making network, a living mind –
I sat in her shadow, in her kitchen,
her timidity could only inhibit me.
Her eyes watery with all the sorrows of Tasmania,
the wilds, the thumb-marked bridges, the ghosts on windy hills,
and cold streams in a young woman's body –
her shivery nerves.

Kaltjiti/Fregon (Gone free)

Winjun and Raulki /me coming /the lock on/ the shed broken/
'it broken'/
they holding /old peach tins/ Raulki throws his/ smell petrol/
sand soaking/ that stuff /you sniffing/ that petrol/
Winjun throws his/ Raulki's gone/ Winjun laughing/ walks away/
across the sand/ stink of petrol/ nine years old/

Lucy/ white dress/ red sand/

materialist/nomad/meet/ the road/ parts/ a stack /of cars /against/
the sky/ the bush dump/ *Drive/ strives/ for a / total clean/*
washing machine/spins red dust/ fires burning/outside prefabs/

stinking hot/ the cry goes out/up/ wail along/ wail along/
women throw themselves/ flat in the dust/
old man's dead/ people go down to the river/ sit in the dry bed/
the ones watching AFL on video/ stop/ have to go/ whirly whirly moves/
across the compound/ rages at an empty office/ the old man's spirit/
rising up rubbish/ and hurling it/ drink cans and paper plates/
higher than trees/ mission brings a coffin/ strapped in a jeep/
he should be put/in the ground/ hands on knees/
waiting for his spirit to settle/ in the land/

wild boys/ petrol brigade/ old world on fire/
Ian rides a horse/ across the basketball court/ in floodlit air/
he put a fence dropper/ through a window/ to smash the video/
time of initiation/ time to live apart/ when the cops come/ in the grey jeep/
he'll be deep/ in the bush

Children's Paintings

Consider the human form
that children
or the very ancients
make in their art.

It's a stick
with a circle for its head.

They do not add
the falsity of perspective,

there's no psychology
in the blue smile,
or the hank of chariot hair.

The circle is whole.
They begin again
in the mystery.

Wakefield Press is an independent publishing and
distribution company based in Adelaide, South Australia.
We love good stories and publish beautiful books.
To see our full range of books, please visit our website at
www.wakefieldpress.com.au
where all titles are available for purchase.
To keep up with our latest releases and news,
subscribe to the Wakefield Weekly at
https://mailchi.mp/wakefieldpress/subscribe

Find us!

Facebook: www.facebook.com/wakefield.press
Instagram: www.instagram.com/wakefieldpress

www.ingramcontent.com/pod-product-compliance
Ingram Content Group Australia Pty Ltd
76 Discovery Rd, Dandenong South VIC 3175, AU
AUHW021239101025
417868AU00001B/1

9 781923 388215